Shapes

written by
Kathleen Urmston and Karen Evans

illustrated by
Dennis Graves

KAEDEN ❤ BOOKS™

Table of Contents

Square

Here is a **square**.

Circle

Here is a **circle**.

Triangle

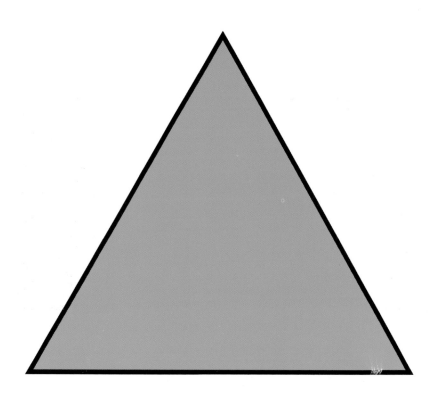

Here is a **triangle**.

Rectangle

Here is a **rectangle**.

Diamond

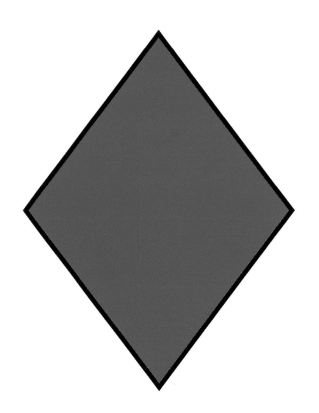

Here is a **diamond**.

Oval

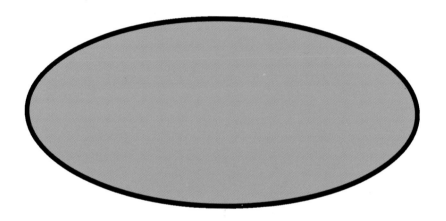

Here is an **oval**.

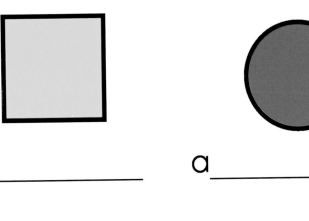

a_____

a_____

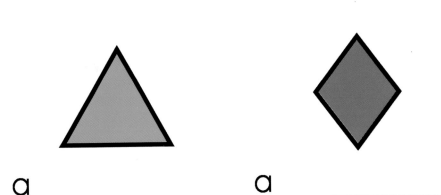

a_____

a_____

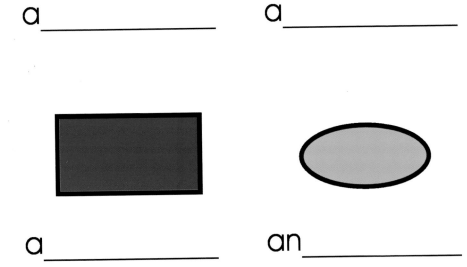

a_____

an_____

Glossary

circle – a shape that is round

diamond – shaped like a kite

oval – shaped like an egg

rectangle – a shape with two long sides and two short sides

shape – the form of an object

square – a shape with four equal sides

triangle – a shape with three sides

Index